Things We Carry

poems by .

Stacy Julin

Finishing Line Press
Georgetown, Kentucky

Things We Carry

ACKNOWLEDGMENTS

Grateful acknowledgment is made to the editors of the following
publications in which these poems first appeared.

Oyster River Pages: "Inheritance"
Word Fountain: "Breadcrumbs," "Superimposed"
Southern Quill: "Almost," "Earthborn," "Praise," "Wound Care"
Sweet Tree Review: "Old Walls"
Exponent 11: "The Middle"
Sky Island Journal: "Mentor"
Pirene's Fountain: "Shedding Skin"
borrowed solace: "Turning"
Tiger's Eye: "Kindred Incantations," "Annie's Men," "Flag Patches," "Chasing
Inspiration"
Finishing Line Press: "A Love for Loneliness"

Publisher: Leah Huete de Maines
Editor: Christen Kincaid
Cover Art: Marianne Goodell
Author Photo: Marc Whiting
Cover Design: Elizabeth Maines McCleavy

Order online: www.finishinglinepress.com
also available on amazon.com

Author inquiries and mail orders:
Finishing Line Press
PO Box 1626
Georgetown, Kentucky 40324
USA

Contents

Inheritance

Childbirth was
a whispered secret,
passed to a long line of young ears
until it no longer resembled itself.

Pushing him out
with the strength of my own muscles,
into the cold open light
of too many voices.

My trembling body
was covered by a warm blanket.
Like the weather outside,
this bleeding went away
after a few weeks.

And I learned to feed him,
but he already knew
how to consume parts of me
with a smile.

What can I give him
that will not be heavy?
It should be the right piece
of myself.
Small enough not to cast
a shadow.

Kindred Incantations

I tried a spell when I was ten.
A penny coined in my birth year,
the name of my admired
and my mother's perfume.

Sealed them in a plastic terrarium
from a cereal box
meant to sprout seeds.
I held it in my hands,
said some words, hid it away.

Secrets unknown to me then
of our grandmothers
who would add a drop
of menstrual blood
to their husband's morning coffee.
An incantation to keep them faithful.

Pennies in perfume.
Red circles in dark drink.

Breadcrumbs

A blue umbrella
from my aunt's favorite drink,

a smooth purple rock
from the dirt
in the canyon.

My painted heart locket
on a silver chain,

scattered through drawers,
boxes of our house.

Their magic will not be inherited
by those who come after,

nor secrets opened
to the unknowing eye.

If they are spread out
on the ground,
like a trail of breadcrumbs,

no one else
can follow them home.

Day Dreaming

My mother told me not to daydream.
"I know you love Grandma, but she's a dreamer.
Stay in reality,
day dreaming does no good."

Still, my grandma painted forests
with water colors,

and she could play songs on the piano
that she dreamed in her sleep.

She read a book to me
with a picture of little girls with red hair
like mine,

poems that stayed with me
and filled my dreams with words.

I felt my heart move when we read
from those books.

She had lived alone most of her life,
but she could create lovely things.

I know why grandma day dreamed.

Annie's Men

She liked to cut out
paper dolls,
keep them orderly
in a box.

When I was twelve,
with curtains closed
against the evening light,
she told the paper dolls
and me
about men.

About cheaters being born,
some people
someday,
getting their dues.

How there were
no new men,
only copies
of old ones.

Advised me not to give away
my insides,
or believe what lips
might say.

She knew what to do
with her men,
curtains closed
against the evening light.

But in the morning,
in the new,
they were never
where she had
left them.

Flag Patches

She always told me to smile,
be nice
even though my hand shook
like a curtain over an open window,
as I held it out with a dollar.

Leery of the man
who handed a pencil back
to me.
His cut-off shorts
with no legs in them.
A flag patch stitched
on one flat side.

My parents had lived through war,
knew about it.
The way it carved people up
inside and out.
Knew it like a song
you wish to forget.

They sat next to,
joked with their friends
who came home
without body parts.

Told me stories about paper
black and white faces,
smiling in uniforms.
Their laughter and tears
blurred and running
like frost on a warm window.

He must have seen it,
fear in my eight-year-old eyes.
A reaction as familiar
as breath.
My mother standing behind me,
seeing another face in his.
But I didn't lower my eyes.

Because you can't, can you?
Look away from a guy
with a flag
and no legs,
selling pencils on the corner.

My Mother's Father

He was married four times,
and buried alone.
Fittingly, some would say.

He liked root beer floats and pistachios,
I tell them when they ask
about the grave we have come to visit.
Mom, what else?
We come here with flowers all the time.

I show them a photo.
We belong in the picture,
except my red hair against his dark hair.
He's wearing a familiar shirt
which always had caramels
in the pockets.
I'm sitting on his knee,
smiling with my drum.
Of all the gifts to give a little girl,
Mom had said.

She was his favorite child,
followed him everywhere,
before seeing him with
the women
who were not her mother.

Mom asked me to bring flowers
each year to him,
before she died.
She couldn't stand the thought
of his grave not cared for.

My boys often run down the hill
at the cemetery,
while I talk to the buried man.
I wish I knew what happened
to that drum.

Almost

If not for God
and penicillin,
life would have been
hours long.
As a moth lives,
young and oblivious.

Dreams,
ambitions—
like the snowflakes,
were too delicate
on a window.
Melting before I could
touch them.

The watching stars
must have made bets,
popped popcorn
to watch these almost moments,
like a predictable football game.

If I could see it laid out,
with the warning of big bumps,
like a topographical map,
I might hide underground
in fear of the coming.

Better to be like the moth,
who flies in the light,
not knowing.

Old Walls

I drove myself to
our old house today
to look at my past.

There is a park behind it,
where there used to be hills
of grass
big enough to lay behind
and fire toy guns
at each other.

I parked facing North
in a carefully chosen space,
mostly hidden
by the large green dumpster.

They were sitting out
in the backyard
with their baby on a blanket,
spread out under my apple tree.

I don't like them still
for paying less than the house
was worth.
Arguing the details
of my memories.

And admit how much I enjoyed
knowing the secrets.
Watching them there,
not belonging.

Oblivious to what really lives
in the crawl space.

And how they were bare-legged,
eating their ham sandwiches
3 feet above
the decomposed body
of my Shetland Sheepdog.

The house
without me,
won't tell them.

Superimposed

The trees had only to grow
a few more feet,
once the last human
was gone.

Reach over the top
and remind the barn
of it's origin,
tribe.

Those broken walls
were never strong enough
to keep a life within them,
or keep the wild out.

Wood spit out nails
and returned to those
waiting.

They came together
as soon as it was dark
and silent.

Grew untrained,
unwatched,
a new generation.

Their dried up leaves
and seeds,
a reminder
of their tryst,
on the impenetrable floor.

A Love for Loneliness

They were hours
I've lost track of now.
Those you glimpse
in dreams
but lose in light
of morning.

Long days
on end
in the bluish hue.
Loneliness sat with me
awhile,
then laid with me
in bed.

I let him stay
longer each visit,
unafraid
and even accustomed
to the silence he brought
as a gift.

Like the cold
that curled around me
from my cracked window,
he wrapped around my grief
and lived beside me,
until we both
longed for days
when blood was warm.

Chasing Inspiration

Among the leaves
swirling in the wind,
go my thoughts,
and I run
far away
to catch them.

They slow down,
hover there.
I reach with both hands,
but they blow
farther away.

I turn to give up,
drop my hands down,
empty.
And then like a nudge,
one small leaf
on my shoulder.

The Middle

Watering your flowers today
at the cemetery

it was so quiet.
We decided to walk.

The kids picked up
cherry tree blossoms
to leave on graves

in the old section.
We read headstones of those
dead one hundred years.

We were there
on the path,

strangely together—
the boys running ahead,
you and dad in the ground.

And me walking
somewhere in between.

Earthborn

Perfection in…

the earth-blown glass,
coating the smallest details
of a tree in wintertime.

the sunshine held
soft and pink,
inside the clouds of early morning.

the lines and crevices
in a child's hand,
tracing the path of what may come.

Praise

He made me,
but do these words
praise Him?
Or wrap around the sky,
foolish as a discarded
fishing net,
always asking why.

Mentor

Traces of you run long,
thin through my creations.

Transparent to others
yet I recognize their fine weave.

Your words form the rivulets
for mine to run down.

Though I live with words,
there are none to describe
the way you are within me.

Bandages

There are a stack of bandages
on our bathroom sink.
Cut out carefully to fit a sore
which won't heal.

He grew up in a dark house
with linoleum floors.
Raised by people who did not
look in their closets.
Never ate dinner together,
and when they talked,
it was often about the weather.

No amount of time,
or pleading,
will erase that house,
or change his belief
that all bleeds
are treated with bandages.

Wound Care

Wanting him filled me up
with an insatiable need to fix
what was wrong.

Holding bandages on seeping wounds,
inflicted before me.

A tiring effort
to stop the good
from bleeding out
with the rest.

My own blister
hardened with the days,
years of things
spilling through.

When it was finally lanced,
what remained was slow,
thick,
yellow.

Shedding Skin

I don't know, the doctor told her.
Laser treatments are painful,
there are so many.
And there would be scarring.
You should think about that.
But she didn't.
Wanted only to shimmy herself
between two cutting edges,
leaving the shell of tattooed skin
behind in one whole piece
like a snake.
Behind closed eyelids, she remembered
how she once craved the pain
of her sewn on colors.
But that could go away
after the shedding.
Her body pink,
naked, and slippery.
Renewed as one born
of water.

Turning

Your world turns
like the merry-go-round
you once cried to
get off of.

My arms are waiting
for you still.

Can you see me
in your spinning?
I'm holding onto ground.
Trying to plant a piece
of you,

so you can root
and stay in the sun.

Walking Counterclockwise

I just noticed it today.

That I put my left shoe
on first,

take the long way home,
and walk counterclockwise.

I will pay more
to avoid the crowds,
every time.

I prefer the soft peaceful moon
to the heat of the sun,

and winter is my favorite season.

Faith

The jump usually comes
before the cushion.
I've tried to learn to jump
and know there will be something under me
when I get to the ground.

Snapshots

Collecting photos to preserve
my tender memories,

your first smile as you
wake up,

The way your tongue sits
out of your mouth,

slightly to the side,
as you draw.

Dreaming sometimes
that I can't find you,

you've been lost
in a place with too many people.

Waking up,
heart pounding,

and then
finding you in your bed.

I wonder about when I am old
and you have gone,

and your room no longer
down the hall.

Will I find comfort
in these pictures?

Or will I,
mind clouded with dementia,
run from room to room each night—

searching for you?

The World After

How will it happen…
the world after this?

The one who wears death's cloak
must be female.
Who better to know
the way home
than she who brought us here?

Will my mother come for me,
open the earth
in Spring
to take me home,
like Demeter took Persephone
from Hades?

Will we know then
who we have been
since before there was night
and then day?

Additional Acknowledgments

I am thankful to God, who gave me my love of poetry, and parents who encouraged it and believed in me.

I am grateful to David, biblical, who wrote the best prose ever.

Loving thanks to my husband Marc, and our children, who are always my inspiration.

Deep gratitude to the many friends in poetry groups who taught me, for Colette Jonopulos and JoAn Osborne of Tiger's Eye Press, for publishing my first chapbook, Finishing Line Press for publishing my second chapbook, and also this one.

A special thank you to Lana Hechtman Ayers for guiding and helping me along the way.

Thanks to Ami Kaye and Lana Hechtman Ayers for their wonderful words on the cover of my book.

Thank you to Marianne Velis Goodell for the beautiful painting on the cover, *Survivor*.

Thanks to all the staff at Finishing Line Press, for giving this manuscript a home.

Stacy Julin's work has been published in *Oyster River Pages, Pirene's Fountain, Sky Island Journal, Southern Quill, Word Fountain,* and has been nominated for a Pushcart Prize. She is the author of two poetry chapbooks, *A Pebble Thrown in Water,* published by Tiger's Eye Press, and *Visiting Ghosts and Ground* from Finishing Line Press (which was published under the name Stacy W. Dixon). She lives with her family at the base of the beautiful Wasatch Mountains.

.